Firefighter

Published in the United States of America by Cherry Lake Publishing
Ann Arbor, Michigan
www.cherrylakepublishing.com

Reading Adviser: Marla Conn MS, Ed., Literacy specialist, Read-Ability, Inc.
Book Design: Jennifer Wahi
Illustrator: Jeff Bane

Photo Credits: © Arisha Ray Singh / Shutterstock.com, 5; © Monkey Business Images / Shutterstock.com, 7, 11, 23;
© Robert Pernell / Shutterstock.com, 9; © Prath / Shutterstock.com, 13; © S-F / Shutterstock.com, 15;
© Michaelpuche / Shutterstock.com, 17; © Fotocrisis / Shutterstock.com, 19; © Tyler Olson / Shutterstock.com, 21;
© aleksandr-mansurov-ru, 2-3, 24; Cover, 1, 8, 16, 22, Jeff Bane

Library of Congress Cataloging-in-Publication Data

Names: Bell, Samantha, author. | Bane, Jeff, 1957- illustrator.
Title: Firefighter / Samantha Bell ; [illustrated by Jeff Bane].
Description: Ann Arbor, Michigan : Cherry Lake Publishing, [2017] | Series:
   My friendly neighborhood | Audience: K to grade 3.
Identifiers: LCCN 2016056585| ISBN 9781634728270 (hardcover) | ISBN
   9781634729161 (pdf) | ISBN 9781534100053 (pbk.) | ISBN 9781534100947
   (hosted ebook)
Subjects: LCSH: Fire fighters--Juvenile literature.
Classification: LCC HD8039.F5 B447 2018 | DDC 363.37092--dc23
LC record available at https://lccn.loc.gov/2016056585

Printed in the United States of America
Corporate Graphics

About the author: Samantha Bell has written and illustrated over 60 books for children. She lives in South Carolina with her family and pets. She is very thankful for the helpers in her community.

About the illustrator: Jeff Bane and his two business partners own a studio along the American River in Folsom, California, home of the 1840 Gold Rush. When Jeff's not sketching or illustrating for clients, he's either swimming or kayaking in the river to relax.

Firefighters are called **first responders**. They come fast to help.

They put out fires. They help those who are hurt. They **rescue** people.

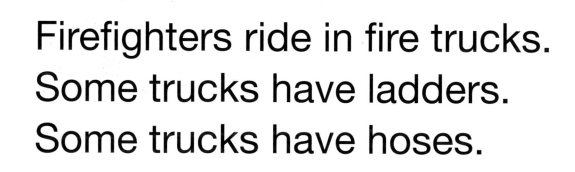

Firefighters ride in fire trucks.
Some trucks have ladders.
Some trucks have hoses.

What color is a fire truck?

A firefighter's job is full of danger.

Firefighters wear helmets and special suits. They help keep the firefighters safe.

Some firefighters work to **prevent** fires. They check alarms. They teach people what to do in case of a fire.

Some firefighters **investigate**.
They find out what started a fire.

What can start a fire?

Firefighters work hard. Sometimes they live at the station. They are always ready to go.

Firefighters take care of the fire truck. They check the hoses. They make sure things work.

Firefighters must be strong.
They exercise. They stay fit.

Firefighters save lives.

What would you like to ask a firefighter?

glossary

first responders (FURST ri-SPAHND-ers) people whose job is to show up first in an emergency

investigate (in-VES-ti-gate) to study something by looking at it closely and asking questions

prevent (pri-VENT) to stop something from happening

rescue (RES-kyoo) to save someone who is in danger

index